PHONICS
READING PROGRAM

Short-Vowels Activity Book

BOOK 11
Short Vowels

Published by Scholastic Inc., *Publishers since 1920*. SCHOLASTIC and associated logos
are trademarks and/or registered trademarks of Scholastic Inc. All rights reserved.

The publisher does not have any control over and does not assume
any responsibility for author or third-party websites or their content.

This book is a work of fiction. Names, characters, places, and incidents are either the product of the
author's imagination or are used fictitiously, and any resemblance to actual persons, living or dead,
business establishments, events, or locales is entirely coincidental.

ISBN: 978-1-338-57294-0

10 9 8 7 6 5 4 3 2 1   19 20 21 22 23

Printed in Malaysia   106

First printing, 2019

Book design by Marissa Asuncion

Scholastic Inc.

Short Vowels

There are 26 letters in the alphabet. Five letters are vowels. They are **a**, **e**, **i**, **o**, and **u**. Every word needs a vowel. Say the short-vowel sound of each letter. Trace the letter with your finger. Then write the letter on the line.

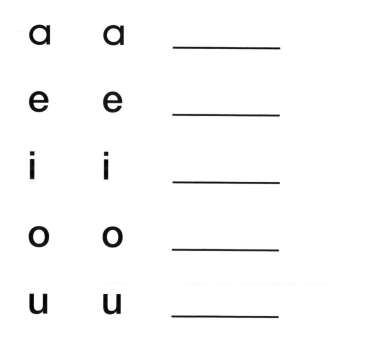

a   a   _____

e   e   _____

i   i   _____

o   o   _____

u   u   _____

Short-Vowel Words

Read the words below aloud. Circle the words that have a short-vowel sound. Put an X on the words that have a long-vowel sound.

can	not	have
pop	peek	keep
know	show	when
with	stop	go
little	friend	truck

Short -a

Woody has to get back to his friends, but which way should he go? Help Woody find his pals. Draw a line along the correct path by following words that have the **short -a** sound.

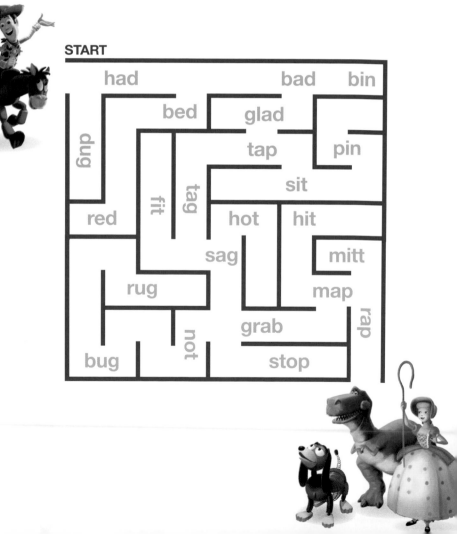

START

had		bad	bin
bed	glad		
bug	tap	pin	
	sit		
red	fit tag	hot	hit
	sag	mitt	
rug		map	
	not	grab	rap
bug		stop	

Short -a

Woody and the other toys are part of Andy's family. Did you know words have families, too? Words that have the same spelling patterns are  called word families. Words like *car*, *far*, and *star* are all in the –ar word family.
Can you make two new words for each word family below? Write a letter in front of each word family.

man	____an	____an
cat	____at	____at
glad	____ad	____ad
nap	____ap	____ap

Short -e

Read each **short -e** word aloud. Draw a line to match each pair of rhyming words.

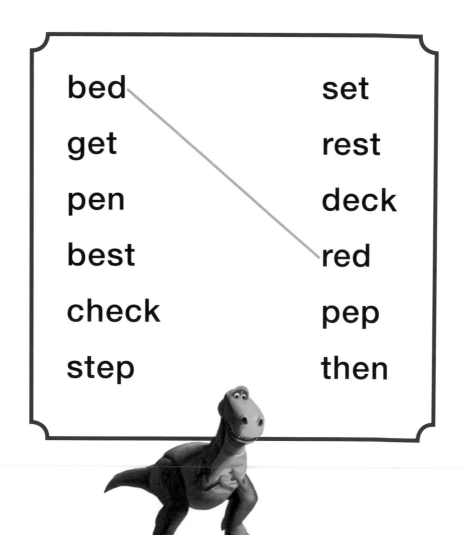

bed	set
get	rest
pen	deck
best	red
check	pep
step	then

Short -e

Circle the following **short -e** words in the puzzle below.

bet	check	get	help	let
next	red	step	wet	when

C	H	O	S	T	R
H	E	G	T	P	E
E	L	E	E	B	D
C	P	T	P	E	W
K	C	L	E	T	E
N	E	X	T	Q	T
G	V	W	H	E	N

Short -i

Bo Peep is playing hide-and-seek. Can she fit all her sheep in the box? You can play along, too. Which **short -i** words fit in the boxes below? Write the correct letter in each box.

| bit | dip | his | in | it | trip |

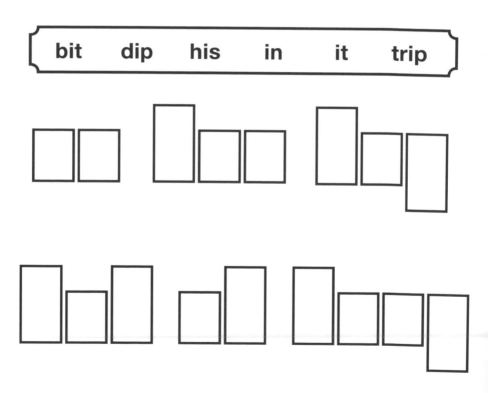

Short -i

Look at the words in the word box.

fish **little** **river** **spill** **will** **wish**

Unscramble the letters to make each word found in the word box. These words have the **short -i** sound.

sihw ＿ ＿ ＿ ＿

hisf ＿ ＿ ＿ ＿

liwl ＿ ＿ ＿ ＿

lslpi ＿ ＿ ＿ ＿ ＿

ellitt ＿ ＿ ＿ ＿ ＿ ＿

erirv ＿ ＿ ＿ ＿ ＿

Short -o

Woody and the other toys are part of Andy's family. Did you know words have families, too? Words that have the same spelling patterns are called word families. Look at the **short -o** word families below. Fill in the blanks with letters to make **short –o** words.

_____ot

_____ot

_____ot

_____op

_____op

_____op

Short =o

Woody likes to ride **on** his horse. What do you like to ride **on**? Draw a picture of it.

I like to ride on a _____.

Short -u

Look at the picture. Complete the sentence with one of the **short -u** words below.

bug	hug	run	tug

Woody gave Hamm a big _____.

Twitch looks like a big, green _____.

The sheep _____ on the rope.

Jessie can _____ fast.

The Little Green Aliens look a lot alike. Rhyming words sound a lot alike because they have the same ending sound. Draw a line to match the rhyming words below.

sun	cut
but	bump
up	duck
truck	dust
jump	pup
must	fun

Short Vowels

Each word below is missing a short vowel. Do you know which one? Fill in the missing letter. Write the complete word next to it. Read each word aloud.

th__t   __ __ __ __

w__th   __ __ __ __

g__t   __ __ __

h__ve   __ __ __ __

m__st   __ __ __ __

st__p   __ __ __ __

get   have   must   stop   that   with

Short-Vowel Words

Some words written backward make another word. For instance, the word *top* written backward spells *pot*. Write the words below backward. Read the words aloud.

tap <u>p</u> <u>a</u> <u>t</u>

tab __ __ __

pit __ __ __

mug __ __ __

nap __ __ __

One of the toys has a second name that reads the same forward and backward.
Who is it?

_____

Answers

Page 2

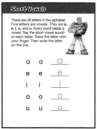

Short Vowels

There are 26 letters in the alphabet. Five letters are vowels. They are a, e, i, o, and u. Every word needs a vowel. Say the short-vowel sound of each letter. Trace the letter with your finger. Then write the letter on the line.

a a <u>a</u>
e e <u>e</u>
i i <u>i</u>
o o <u>o</u>
u u <u>u</u>

Page 3

Short-Vowel Words

Read the words below aloud. Circle the words that have a short-vowel sound. Put an X on the words that have a long-vowel sound.

can	not	have
pop	peek	keep
know	snow	when
with	stop	go
little	friend	truck

Page 4

Short -a

Woody has to get back to his friends, but which way should he go? Help Woody find his pals. Draw a line along the correct path by following words that have the short -a sound.

Page 5

Short -a

Woody and the other toys are part of Andy's family. Did you know words have families, too? Words that have the same spelling patterns are called word families. Words like car, far, and star are all in the -ar word family. Can you make two new words for each word family below? Write a letter in front of each word family.

-an	-at	-ad	-ap
ban	bat	bad	cap
can	fat	cad	gap
fan	hat	dad	lap
pan	mat	fad	map
ran	pat	had	pap
tan	rat	lad	rap
van	sat	mad	sap
	vat	pad	tap
		sad	zap
		tad	

Page 6

Short -e

Read each short -e word aloud. Draw a line to match each pair of rhyming words.

bed	set
get	rest
pen	deck
best	red
check	pep
step	then

Page 7

Short -e

Circle the following short -a words in the puzzle below.

bet   check   get   help   let
next   red   step   wet   when

C	H	O	S	T	R
H	E	G	T	P	E
E	L	E	E	B	D
C	P	T	P	E	W
K	C	L	E	T	E
N	E	X	T	Q	T
G	V	W	H	E	N

Page 8

Short -i

Bo Peep is playing hide-and-seek. Can she fit all her sheep in the box? You can play along, too. Which short -i words fit in the boxes below? Write the correct letter in each box.

bit   dip   his   in   it   trip

in his dip

bit it trip

Page 9

Short -i

Look at the words in the word box.

fish   little   river   spill   will   wish

Unscramble the letters to make each word found in the word box. These words have the short -i sound.

sihw   w i s h
hsif   f i s h
liwl   w i l l
lslpi   s p i l l
ellitt   l i t t l e
erirv   r i v e r

Page 10

Short -o

Woody and the other toys are part of Andy's family. Did you know words have families, too? Words that have the same spelling patterns are called word families. Fill in the blanks with letters to make short -o words.

-ot	-op
cot	bop
dot	cop
got	hop
hot	lop
jot	mop
lot	pop
not	sop
pot	top
rot	
tot	

Page 12

Short -u

Look at the picture. Complete the sentence with one of the short -u words below.

bug   hug   run   tug

Woody gave Hamm a big <u>hug</u>.

Twitch looks like a big, green <u>bug</u>.

The sheep <u>tug</u> on the rope.

Jessie can <u>run</u> fast.

Page 13

Short -u

The Little Green Aliens look a lot alike. Rhyming words sound a lot alike because they have the same ending sound. Draw a line to match the rhyming words below.

sun	cut
but	bump
up	duck
truck	dust
jump	pup
must	fun

Page 14

Short Vowels

Each word below is missing a short vowel. Do you know which one? Fill in the missing letter. Write the complete word next to it. Read each word aloud.

th_t   <u>t h a t</u>
w_th   <u>w i t h</u>
g_t   <u>g e t</u>
h_ve   <u>h a v e</u>
m_st   <u>m u s t</u>
st_p   <u>s t o p</u>

get   have   must   stop   that   with

Page 15

Short-Vowel Words

Some words written backward make another word. For instance, the word tap written backward reads pat. Write the words below backward. Then write the word.

tap   <u>p a t</u>
tab   <u>b a t</u>
pit   <u>t i p</u>
mug   <u>g u m</u>
nap   <u>p a n</u>

One of the toys has a second name that reads the same forward and backward. Who is it?

_____